101 Cycling Programmes

Enhance your fitness both indoors and outdoors, for beginners and experienced cyclists

By Thomas W Gibson

ISBN: 9781520401966

Table of Contents

Disclaimer

This book is not meant to be used, nor should it be used, to diagnose or treat any medical problems. For diagnosis or treatment of any medical problems, consult your own physician. The publisher and author are not responsible for any specific health or allergy needs that may require medical supervision and are not liable for any damages or negative consequences from any fitness session within this book. I recommend consulting your doctor to assess and/or identify any health-related issues prior to completing training sessions within this book which are of a higher difficulty level.

Thank You

I would like to thank you for purchasing this book. I hope that you find it useful and you gain many health benefits from the programmes and ideas provided. If you enjoy the content, I would appreciate it greatly if you left a review on Amazon, as it helps spread the word of this book.

Many thanks again, and I hope you enjoy!

Introduction to 101 Cycling Programmes

Why Cycling?

Cycling is a growing sport, especially within the UK, with more than 2 million estimated to be cycling at least once a week as of 2015. This is likely due to the increased presence within the media, as a form of transportation, being able to get out and see the countryside, and the many health benefits associated with the exercise.

What is this book for?

This book will look to give guidance and ideas to those looking to use cycling as a method to improve fitness through the supplied sessions. It is aimed at all ends of the cycling spectrum, from those starting out on their first cycling exploits, those looking to find the commute to work a little less tiresome, people preparing for their first 100 mile sportive, or cyclists looking to win Time Trials, Road Races, Hill Climbs, etc. Sessions provided span from 10 minutes up to 2 hours+.

How to use this book?

The 101 programmes provided in this book are divided into three main methods of rating effort: heart rate, power, and rated perceived exertion. This will allow each programme to be accessible to the novice cyclist beginning in the sport to the advanced cyclist looking for new programme ideas. It will not, unfortunately, go into the details of periodisation of long term training plans and is simply a collection of varied programmes.

Locations

With cycling now accessible to a much wider spectrum of people and training locations, the provided programmes aim to be both applicable to the indoor training environment using stationary bikes/turbo trainers, as well as to the outdoors on mountain bikes, road bikes, cyclocross bikes, commuter bikes, etc.

1

Terminology

The following definitions will give a brief insight into terms used throughout the book

Climbing

Climbing in cycling is used to describe when heading up a hill or a mountain. It is on the mountains where the cycling grand tours such as tour de France and Giro d'Italia are won. If you watch cycling, you have most likely noticed that the majority of climbs are won by slight individuals. This is due to the advantage provided by being light simply because there is less weight to pull up the mountain

Sprinting

This is most commonly seen at the end of bike races, but also when individuals are racing each other up the hills and mountains. These situations are usually the most physically demanding periods and can only be sustained at full pace for around 1 to 3 minutes.

Functional Threshold

This is the best effort you are able to ride for around 45 to 60 minutes at a time. Usually given as a number in power (i.e. what average watts you can sustain) or heart rate (i.e. what average heart rate you can sustain). Regular assessment of this figure is a good method of monitoring your fitness progress and is regularly used to determine training zones.

Sweet spot

This is a named training zone at around 90% of a person's functional threshold power or heart rate. It is an intensity of training where you may gain the best training value from your time. It allows your body to manage lactate (lactic acid) most effectively and not be too intense to require extended recovery periods.

VO2 Max

This is the maximum rate your body (heart, lungs and muscles) can use oxygen during intense exercise over one minute. The more oxygen you can take in, the more energy that can be produced in your muscles. It is commonly tested and then used as an indicator of fitness, and it is measured using the maximum amount of oxygen an athlete can utilise per minute per kilogram of body weight. Dividing the amount of oxygen by the rider's weight allows for comparison between individuals. VO2 max is usually around 110-120% of your FTP.

Aerobic

This is a form of energy system within the body that utilises oxygen to help produce the energy required during low-medium intensity exercise. This system produces large amounts of energy but a slow speed. The oxygen is required to help breakdown carbohydrates and/or fats, which are used in the production of energy required for muscle contraction. When working within the aerobic energy system, there is typically enough glucose to fuel cycling for 3 hours or more.

Anaerobic

This is a form of energy system within the body where oxygen is not required to produce energy. The period of this energy system can usually only last for around 3 minutes at the most. This form of energy system creates more energy much quicker than the aerobic system, but it uses much more energy. This tires quickly and cannot be used for long periods of time, and it also gives the trademark burning legs due to excessive accumulation of lactate in the muscles used. However, simply reducing effort levels will allow for the removal of this product quickly.

High Intensity Interval Training (HIIT)

This is a form of training that is usually relatively short in duration due to the high intensity nature. Short bursts of high intensity anaerobic efforts (5s to 3 minutes) are used followed by periods of rest that are usually shorter than the work period. This form of trainings benefits are thought to include improving our cardiovascular system and muscular power, but the biggest benefit is the short time periods required for these adaptations.

Recovery

This is an underrated aspect of fitness training; it is in this period that physiological adaptations of training are made. The act of training merely produces the stimulus within our bodies to allow for the adaptations required for improvements in fitness. If recovery is not allowed, your body will become fatigued and struggle to produce the required stimulus for physiological adaptations. The best way to prevent fatigue is to progressively increase your level of training rather than having sudden increases. Morning resting heart rate level can be used to monitor fatigue (if HR is raised above normal, this may suggest fatigue), and a general subjective feeling may also be used.

Cadence (RPM)

This is the most common cycling term used to measure how fast your legs are pedalling. Most indoor trainers will show this on their screen. On outdoor bikes, sensors can be bought to show this data but will also require some form of cycling computer to display this. Typically cyclists will pedal at around 75-100 RPM.

Cycling computers

These devices are extremely common on the majority of bikes seen on the road, costing from as little as £40 up to around £350. Basic units provide information such as speed, average speed, and distance. The more expensive models allow tracking and recording of distance (via GPS), power and HR (when paired with an HR belt and power meter), cadence, etc. Recording will allow you to view and evaluate your data after the ride via popular sites such as 'Garmin Connect' and 'Strava'. Indoor trainers now commonly come equipped with cycling computers, but these usually only show real-time data, meaning it usually cannot be recorded to view later.

Bib Shorts

Bib shorts come as a highly recommended piece of clothing if you are intending to spend a lot of time training on a bike. Getting used to a saddle can be an uncomfortable process, and the padding provided through bib shorts goes a long way toward negating this issue. They are also lightweight and breathable, meaning you will be less likely to become overheated during exercise. Compared to standard padded shorts, bib shorts have straps that keep the pad in place, meaning you are not regularly re-arranging.

2

Heart Rate Zones

What is Heart Rate (HR)

HR is essentially the amount of times your heart beats in one minute and is an indicator of how hard your body is working. In other words, the higher the HR, the more you are working.

What are HR zones?

These zones can be used to gauge how hard you are working and allow you to plan your cycling session difficulties. These zones are based upon the maximum heart rate you can produce. In order to use your HR to monitor your training, you will require an HR monitor which now can be picked up for as little as £30.

Measuring Max HR

The simplest way of finding your maximum heart rate is simply by using the formula below:

Men: 214 - (0.8 x age)

Women: 209 - (0.9 x age)

A more precise method of finding your HR max would be:

- Easy 10-15 minutes pedalling

- 5 minutes riding at a hard pace

- 5 minutes riding at an easy pace

- 5 minutes riding at a hard pace

- 5 minutes riding at an easy pace

- 20 minutes riding as hard as possible

This should allow you to reach your maximum HR within the 20 minute block.

3
Power Zones + Power Meters

What is power (watts)?

Power is the amount of force and velocity supplied to the pedals during cycling and this force is expressed as a watt. Power meter training popularity is due to its reliability, and unlike HR, it is not affected by factors such as hydration, sleep, overall muscle fatigue and temperature, which can have a huge impact. This makes power a more accurate gauge of effort than HR.

What are power meters?

A power meter is simply a device attached to your bike, usually within the crank, pedals, or rear wheel hub. Power meters are usually seen on conventional bikes rather than static trainers and indoor bikes. However, they are becoming more readily available in the indoor environment, too.

A power meter will measure the amount of force you provided via strain gauges, and then display this as watts. The speed in which you turn the crank (cadence) and the amount of force you provide are calculated together to show you the watts. This data will be provided via the form of a handlebar-based computer (e.g. a Garmin), which will record your data, allowing you to review it at a later date. Power meters are by far the most expensive method of monitoring effort with top prices of £2000+, costs are quickly coming down with some models now available for around £400, so they are a big investment and if you are looking to buy one, I would suggest much deeper research than the information provided here.

What are power zones?

To train effectively, the correct amount of training load is required to allow the needed physiological adaptations, and the right amount of recovery is required so the body is able to adapt. To quantify intensity, it is common to use power training levels, or "zones". These zones will be described further on in the book in the "Gauging Your Effort" chapter. When using a power meter, these zones will most commonly be derived from your functional threshold power, a term described below.

How to calculate your power zones

The most common method of working out your own individual power zones is to complete a test that will work out your functional threshold (FT). FT is the very best effort you can sustain for one hour of non-stop riding. This can be tested without having to complete 1 hour of 100% riding, through the same method shown above for maximum HR. Once the test has been completed (as mentioned before, this test will have needed to be recorded to have your average power), work out the average power for the final 20 minutes of hard riding. Next, multiply the number by 0.95, which will give you your FT. This calculation can also be applied to your HR average for 20 minutes to provide an FT HR.

4
Rated Perceived Exertion

What is perceived exertion?

Rated Perceived Exertion (RPE) is a method of measuring how much effort, or intensity, you use during a particular effort. For example, 0 would be used to describe how easy you would feel laying down or sitting in a chair, and 10 would be described for how you feel at the end of a maximum fitness test. This method is used in many different sports and is based on the Borg Scale.

This is the easiest method of knowing which training zone you are in, as it requires no equipment and money. For the purpose of this book, each individual session will be broken down into RPEs within sessions.

How to use perceived exertion

10 Point RPE scale	
0	Rest
1	Really Easy
2	Easy
3	Moderate
4	Moderate +
5	Hard
6	Hard +
7	Really Hard
8	Really Hard +
9	Extremely Hard
10	Maximal

5

Gauging Your Effort Table

As mentioned above, throughout this book's programmes, all efforts will be linked to the table below. Each programme will have suggested zones for each stage of the session. The zone provided is only a guide; if it is too hard, feel free to drop to the appropriate level, or if too easy, then move up into the next zone.

Zone	RPE	Used in	You should be able to	%MHR	%FTP	%FTP (HR)
1	1-3	Recovery	Sing	< 65%	< 50%	< 65%
2	4-5	Endurance	Chat	70%	56-75%	66-85%
3	6	Tempo	Only just talk	80%	76-90%	86-94%
4	7-8	Long climbs + time trailing	Short Phrases	85%	91-105%	95-105%
5	9	Short climbs	Single words	90%	106-120%	106% +
6	10	Sprinting	Pant	N/A	121-150%	N/A

Zone one – Active recovery

Training zone one is the easiest zone within this book and is predominantly used as a recovery set between intervals. It is a perfect way of keeping your legs spinning without adding any associated fatigue to your body and there will be minimal awareness of effort. It can also be used as a whole session when looking to recover the following day from a particularly hard session.

Zone two – Endurance

Riding in this zone can last from 3 hours to up to 7 hours for professional cyclists, but anyone reading this book is likely unable to give that time period to cycling for such little gain. Often described as an 'all day' pace, riding in this zone will promote your body to use fat as a fuel source for riding. This system is in your aerobic energy systems, so it will not produce lactic acid and the associated leg burn, allowing long duration rides.

Zone three – Tempo

Within this zone, an experienced rider would be able to ride for around one to three hours. This zone is often described as being one where a high pace/speed can be maintained, but without the feeling of riding too hard. Riding in zone three promotes storage of glycogen in your muscles. You will be aware of your breathing becoming deeper and more frequent within this zone.

Zone four – Threshold

This zone lay on the point between anaerobic and aerobic energy systems. Due to this zone working at the threshold level, lactic acid is produced, meaning this zone can be held for a limited period of time, from 10 minutes to 1 hour. Training in this zone pushes a rider's ability to work for longer in an anaerobic energy state. A one-hour time trial would take place in this zone. Normal conversation becomes difficult within this zone.

Zone five – VO2

This is an effort you are most likely only able to hold for between 3 to 8 minutes, usually seen in races when a rider is going full speed up a short climb. Due to intense effort required, max total time within this zone for a ride would likely be around 40 minutes. It is an extremely draining training zone due to the intensity of effort, and due to the short duration able to hold this effort, your HR may not respond until the latter stages.

Zone six – Anaerobic

This is a type of effort you are likely only able to hold for around 2/3 minutes and can be best described as a max effort, seen on the road when cyclists are attacking. The N/An on the above table is because your heart rate will not have time to respond to the effort. Conversation in this zone will not be possible due to the intense nature. Additionally, repeated day-to-day sessions are usually not completed due to an inadequate time for recovery.

6

Programmes - 0-15 minutes

Shorter programmes will concentrate on higher intensity efforts in order to achieve a physiological benefit from such a short period. These sessions will mostly resemble HIIT programmes.

No. 1

Duration: 10 minutes.

Improves: Sprinting.

Good for: Strength and power of short durations.

Tip: Pace yourself on the first efforts, otherwise the last efforts will not be nice!

5 Minute Warm-up - Z1/2/3	
15s	Z6
15s	Z0
Repeat x 10	

5 Minute Cool Down - Z1

No. 2

Duration: 11 minutes.

Improves: Sprinting.

Good for: Quick session that will raise your HR and practice Zone 6 work.

Tip: Use the warm-up effectively so you are ready to apply full effort.

3 Minute Warm-Up - Z1/2/3	
20s	Z6
10s	Z0
Repeat x 10	

3 Minute Cool Down - Z1

<u>*No. 3*</u>

Duration: 12 minutes.

Improves: Sprinting.

Good for: Developing Zone 6 power over different durations.

Tip: Stick to recovery times to ensure full ability on sections of effort.

2 Minute Warm-up - Z1/2/3	
15s	Z6
15s Recovery	Z1
30s	Z6
30s Recovery	Z1
45s	Z6
45s Recovery	Z1
1 Minute	Z6
1 Minute Recovery	Z1
15s	Z6
15s Recovery	Z1
30s	Z6
30s Recovery	Z1
45s	Z6
45s Recovery	Z1

2 Minute Cool Down - Z1

No. 4

Duration: 12 minutes.

Improves: Sprinting.

Good for: Developing maximal power over intervals ranging from 15s to 60s.

Tip: If you find this easy, you can simply repeat with a 5 minute rest between sets. The table works from left to right, moving down.

2 Minute Warm-up - Z1/2/3	
Z6	Z1
15s	45s
30s	30s
45s	15s
60s	60s
45s	15s
30s	30s
15s	45s

2 Minute Cool Down - Z1

<u>*No. 5*</u>

Duration: 13 minutes.

Improves: Time trailing.

Good for: Short time periods working in Zone 5.

Tip: Knowing that this is a short session, full effort can be put into each Zone 5/6 effort.

2 Minute Warm-up - Z1/2/3	
3 Minutes	Z5
1:30 Recovery	Z1
2 Minutes	Z5
1 Minute Recovery	Z1
1 Minute	Z5
30s Recovery	Z1
30s	Z6

2 Minute Cool Down - Z1

No. 6

Duration: 13 minutes.

Improves: Long steep climbs.

Good for: Introduction to cadence drills, with small Zone 6 sprints.

Tip: Avoid the lower cadences if you have problematic knees.

2 Minute Warm-up - Z1/2/3	
1 Minute - 90 RPM	Z4
1 Minute - 80 RPM	Z4
1 Minute - 70 RPM	Z4
1 Minute - 60 RPM	Z4
1 Minute - 50 RPM	Z4
1 Minute - 60 RPM	Z4
1 Minute - 70 RPM	Z4
1 Minute - 80 RPM	Z4
1 Minute - 90 RPM	Z4

Add a 5s Zone 6 Sprint Every 2 Minutes

2 Minute Cool Down - Z1

No. 7

Duration: 13 minutes.

Improves: Sprinting.

Good for: Combining Zones 5 + 6 in back-to-back intervals.

Tip: Stick to zones during earlier stages, as the middle portion on the programme will be hard.

1 Minute Warm-up - Z1/2	
3 Minutes	Z3
2 Minutes	Z4
1 Minute	Z5
1 Minute	Z6
1 Minute	Z5
2 Minutes	Z4
3 Minutes	Z3

1 Minute Cool Down - Z1

No. 8

Duration: 13:40 minutes.

Improves: Time Trailing.

Good for: Early introduction to using Z4.

Tip: Aim for the higher end of Zone 4 during intervals.

2 Minute Warm-Up - Z1/2/3	
40s	Z4+
20s Recovery	Z1
40s	Z4+
20s Recovery	Z1
40s	Z5
20s Recovery	Z1
40s	Z5
20s Recovery	Z1
40s	Z5
20s Recovery	Z1
40s	Z5+
20s Recovery	Z1
40s	Z5+
20s Recovery	Z1
40s	Z5+
20s Recovery	Z1
40s	Z5+
20s Recovery	Z1
40s	Z6

2 Minute Cool Down - Z1

No. 9

Duration: 14 minutes.

Improves: Sprinting.

Good for: Maximal Zone 6 efforts.

Tip: Although a difficult session, really put the effort into each sprint effort during every second.

2 Minute Warm-Up - Z1/2/3	
10s Max Sprint	Z6
50s Recovery	Z1
Repeat x 10	

2 Minute Cool Down - Z1

No. 10

Duration: 14 minutes.

Improves: Short length climbing.

Good for: Standing climbing efforts.

Tip: Improve your body's ability to work hard when standing on the bike.

2 Minute Warm-up - Z1/2/3	
45s - Standing	Z5
15s – Seated	Z3
Repeat x 4	
3 Minutes Recovery	Z1
45s - Standing	Z5
15s – Seated	Z3
Repeat x 4	

2 Minute Cool Down - Z1

<u>*No. 11*</u>

Duration: 14 minutes.

Improves: Standing climbing.

Good for: A combination of steep standing climbs and sprinting.

Tip: Make sure you drop a few gears when you start your sprint, otherwise you will find it difficult to turn the pedals quickly for the first few seconds.

2 Minute Warm-up - Z1/2/3	
30s	Z5
30s Standing - 70 RPM or lower	Z5
30s Sprint	Z6
30s Recovery	Z1
Repeat x 5	

2 Minutes Cool Down - Z1

No. 12

Duration: 14 minutes.

Improves: Endurance.

Good for: Intro to cadence drills.

Tip: Aims to acclimatize your body to different cadence speeds for more intense sessions later in the book. Ideal practice could be done on a commute to work.

2 Minute Warm-up - Z1/2/3	
1 Minute - 110 RPM	Z3
1 Minute - 60-70 RPM	Z3
1 Minute - 110 RPM	Z3
1 Minute - 60-70 RPM	Z3
1 Minute - 110 RPM	Z3
1 Minute - 60-70 RPM	Z3
1 Minute - 110 RPM	Z3
1 Minute - 60-70 RPM	Z3
1 Minute - 110 RPM	Z3
1 Minute - 60-70 RPM	Z3

2 Minute Cool Down - Z1

No. 13

Duration: 14 minutes.

Improves: Sprinting.

Good for: Repeated efforts of Zone 6 under progressive fatigue.

Tip: If you think 20 intervals is too much, drop the amount of repetitions.

2 Minute Warm-up - Z1/2/3	
30s	Z6
30s Recovery	Z1
Repeat x 5	
15s	Z6
15s Recovery	Z1
Repeat x 5	
10s	Z6
10s Recovery	Z1
Repeat x 5	
5s	Z6
5s Recovery	Z1
Repeat x 5	

2 Minute Cool Down - Z1

<u>No. 14</u>

Duration: 14:30 minutes.

Improves: Short sprints.

Good for: Maintaining effort while working near maximal intensity.

Tip: Ensure you use the rest period properly so maximum effort can be put into efforts.

2 Minute Warm-up - Z1/2/3	
10s	Z6
20s	Z5
30s	Z4
30s	Z1
Repeat x 8	

2 Minute Cool Down - Z1

No. 15

Duration: 14:30 minutes.

Improves: Repeated sprinting.

Good for: Aims to work on improving repeated Zone 6 ability with little rest between efforts.

Tip: As mentioned before, ensure rest periods are completed so maximum effort can be applied to work periods.

30s	Z6
15s	Z1
Repeat x 4	
2 Minutes Recovery	Z1
1 Minute	Z6
30s	Z1
Repeat 1 Minute and 30s x 3	
2 Minutes Recovery	Z1
30s	Z6
15s	Z1
Repeat 30s and 15s x 4	

No. 16

Duration: 14:30 minutes.

Improves: Time trailing.

Good for: Sustained short efforts with little rest

Tip: Short, difficult efforts followed by short recovery time will quickly overload your body, making the final few efforts feel extremely difficult.

2 Minute Warm-Up - Z1/2/3	
1 Minute	Z5
30s Recovery	Z1
1 Minute	Z5
30s Recovery	Z1
1 Minute	Z5
30s Recovery	Z1
1 Minute	Z5
30s Recovery	Z1
1 Minute	Z5
30s Recovery	Z1
1 Minute	Z5
30s Recovery	Z1
1 Minute	Z5
30s Recovery	Z1

2 Minute Cool Down - Z1

No. 17

Duration: 15 minutes.

Improves: Short climbing.

Good for: Work in multiple training zones with no recovery in transitions.

Tip: Within the 5-minute intervals, aim to progressively move through each zone (i.e. 2 minutes at Zone 4, 2 minutes at Zone 5, 1 minute Zone 6).

1 Minute Warm-up - Z1/2/3	
5 Minutes	Z4/5/6
3 Minutes Recovery	Z1
5 Minutes	Z4/5/6

1 Minute Cool Down - Z1

No. 18

Duration: 15 minutes.

Improves: Time trialing.

Good for: Improving sustained efforts.

Tip: Simply a 15-minute effort as fast/far as possible during the time, you should have given your all by the end. Don't go too hard on the first few minutes or you will drop off heavily over the last few minutes.

15 Minutes	Z4/5

No. 19

Duration: 15 minutes.

Location: Extended sprints.

Good for: Longest duration Zone 6 power.

Tip: This will be an extremely draining session, so allow complete rest between efforts.

2 Minute Warm-up - Z4/5	
1 Minute Recovery	Z0
3 Minutes	Z6
1 Minute Recovery	Z0
3 Minutes	Z6
1 Minute Recovery	Z0
3 Minutes	Z6

1 Minute Cool Down - Z1

No. 20

Duration: 15:30 minutes.

Improves: Time trailing.

Good for: Continuing to work through escalating effort output with no immediate rest following a Z6 effort.

Tip: Aim to stay within zone 3 in the 1 minute interval despite the temptation to go quicker, as you will not be able to commit fully during the zone 5 and 6 intervals.

2 Minute Warm-Up - Z1/2/3	
1 Minute	Z3
45s	Z4
30s	Z5
15s	Z6
30s	Z5
45s	Z4
1 Minute	Z3
2 Minute Rest	Z1
Repeat x 2	

2 Minute Cool Down - Z1

7

Programmes - 16-30 minutes

A combination of long rest periods and lower zones spaced over longer durations increasing your overall cycling time

No. 21

Duration: 18 minutes.

Improves: Cadence efficiency.

Good for: Ability to work at different cadence speeds.

Tip: Complete first two cycles through 30s intervals at Zone 3, the 3rd and 4th cycles through at Zone 4, finally the 5th and 6th intervals at Zone 5.

2 Warm-up - Z1/2	
30s - 50 RPM	Z3 - Z4 - Z5
30s - 60 RPM	Z3 - Z4 - Z5
30s - 70 RPM	Z3 - Z4 - Z5
30s - 80 RPM	Z3 - Z4 - Z5
30s - 90 RPM	Z3 - Z4 - Z5
30s - 100 RPM	Z3 - Z4 - Z5
Repeat x 6	Z3 - Z4 - Z5

Z3 for 1st and 2nd Repetitions, Z4 for 3rd and 4th Repetitions, Z5 for 5th and 6th Repetitions

2 Minute Cool Down - Z1

No. 22

Duration: 19 minutes.

Improves: Short sprints.

Good for: Equal rest to work periods in Zone 5 and 6.

Tip: This is a relatively short session with a good sized rest period halfway through, so really commit to each interval.

2 Minute Warm-up - Z1/2/3	
30s	Z5
30s	Z2
Repeat x 5	
5 Minute Recovery	Z1
30s	Z6
30s	Z1
Repeat 30s Intervals x 5	

2 Minute Cool Down - Z1

No. 23

Duration: 20 minutes.

Improves: Short climbing.

Good for: A quick simple spin working on Zone 4 and 5.

Tip: Remember this short type of session can be completed sandwiched in the middle of an outdoor ride.

2 Minute Warm-up Z2/3	
30s	Z4
30s	Z5
30s Standing	Z5
30s Recovery	Z1
Repeat x 10	

2 Minute Cool Down - Z1

<u>*No. 24*</u>

Duration: 20 minutes.

Improves: Short sprints.

Good for: Zone 6 Tabatta Sprints.

Tip: There will be a large number of repetitions of Zone 6 efforts.

5 Minute Warm-up Z1/2/3	
20s Sprint	Z6
10s Recovery	Z1
Repeat x 20	
5 Minute recovery after 10 Reps	Z1

5 Minute Cool Down - Z1

<u>*No. 25*</u>

Duration: 20 minutes.

Improves: Maximal sprints.

Good for: Large repetition of maximal Zone 6 sprints.

Tip: Start on a slightly lower gear than you'd think so you can quickly get your legs spinning, and then move up the gears.

5 Minute Warm-up - Z1/2/3	
8s	Z6
22s Recovery	Z1
Repeat x 10	
5 Minute Recovery	Z1
8s	Z6
22s Recovery	Z1
Repeat 8s + 22s x 10	

5 Minute Cool Down - Z1

No. 26

Duration: 21 minutes.

Improves: Time trialing and endurance.

Good for: Combination work between Zone 5 and 3.

Tip: Early efforts may seem easy, but as the session moves forward, the lack of rest will gradually cause the difficulty to increase.

5 Minute Warm-up - Z1/2/3	
40s	Z5
30s	Z3
Repeat x 10	

5 Minute Cool Down - Z2/1

No. 27

Duration: 21:25 minutes.

Improves: Time trailing.

Good for: Repeated exposure to Zone 5 intervals.

Tip: Aim to be in the upper limits of this session, as the interval times are not too long for Zone 5 training.

5 Minute Warm-up - Z1/2/3	
45s	Upper Z5
30s	Z1
Repeat x 9	

5 Minute Cool Down - Z1

<u>*No. 28*</u>

Duration: 22 minutes.

Improves: Sprinting.

Good for: Repeatedly working in Zone 6 with no complete rest period.

Tip: Although the first set of efforts will be difficult, commit to the session, as durations gradually get smaller.

5 Minute Warm-up - Z1/2/3	
30s	Z6
20s	Z4
Repeat x 5	
60s Recovery	Z1
25s	Z6
15s	Z4
Repeat x 5	
60s Recovery	Z1
20s	Z6
10s	Z4
Repeat x 5	

5 Minute Cool Down - Z1

<u>*No. 29*</u>

Duration: 24 minutes.

Improves: Short sprints.

Good for: Tabbata intervals.

Tip: If completing an indoor session with such high intensity like this one, try to have a towel and a fan handy, as you will get hot and sweaty.

4 Minute Warm-up - Z1/2/3	
20s	Z6
10s	Z1
Repeat x 8	
4 Minutes Recovery	Z1
40s	Z5
20s	Z1
Repeat 40s & 20s x 8	

4 Minute Cool Down - Z1

<u>*No. 30*</u>

Duration: 25 minutes.

Improves: Ability to ride at high and low cadences.

Good for: Tempo riding through varied cadences.

Tip: If you find riding at a lower cadence produces pain in your knees, simply raise the speed during the lower speed sections.

2 Minute Warm-up - Z1/2/3	
1 min - 120 RPM+	Z4
1 min - 80 RPM-	Z4
1 min - 120 RPM+	Z4
1 min - 80 RPM-	Z4
1 min - 120 RPM+	Z4
1 min - 80 RPM-	Z4
1 min - 120 RPM+	Z4
1 min - 80 RPM-	Z4
5 Minute Recovery	Z1
Repeat Above x 1	

2 Minute Cool Down - Z1

<u>*No. 31*</u>

Duration: 25 minutes.

Improves: Sprinting under fatigue.

Good for: Sustained tempo riding with sprints.

Tip: Ensure during your minute intervals you drop to Zone 4 as opposed to Zone 5, otherwise you will not be able to complete the session.

5 Minute Warm-up - Z1/2/3	
15s	Z6
1 Minute	Z4
15s	Z6
1 Minute	Z4
15s	Z6
1 Minute	Z4
15s	Z6
1 Minute	Z4
5 Minute Recovery	Z1
Repeat Above x 2	

5 Minute Cool Down - Z1

No. 32

Duration: 25 minutes.

Improves: Standing climbing.

Good for: Zone 6 power with a short work time in Zone 3.

Tip: Ensure you are not in Zone 6 in the standing efforts, as this will make the Zone 3 efforts harder to commit to.

5 Minute Warm-up - Z1/2/3	
40s Standing	Z5
20s	Z3
Repeat x 5	
15s Sprint	Z6
15s Recovery	Z1
Repeat x 10	
5 minute Steady Pace	Z3
10s Sprint	Z6
20s Recovery	Z1
Repeat x 10	

5 Minute Cool Down - Z1

No. 33

Duration: 25:05 minutes.

Improves: Sprinting.

Good for: Repeated varied durations of Zone 6 intensity.

Tip: If struggling for the final set of Zone 6 efforts, try dropping to Zone 5.

5 Minute Warm-up - Z1/2/3	
15s	Z6
10s	Z1
Repeat x 5	
2 Minutes Recovery	Z1
40s	Z6
20s	Z1
Repeat 40s and 20s intervals x 3	
2 Minutes Recovery	Z1
15s	Z6
10s	Z1
Repeat 15s and 10s intervals x 4	
2 Minutes Recovery	Z1
40s	Z6
20s	Z1
Repeat 40s and 20s intervals x 2	

5 Minute Cool Down - Z1

<u>*No. 34*</u>

Duration: 26:30 minutes.

Improves: Time trailing and tempo riding.

Good For: Working through training zones with no recovery.

Tip: Move through the effort zones on each individual effort (i.e. on the first two repetitions Zone 4, next two repetitions Zone 5, next two repetitions Zone 6).

5 Minute Warm-up - Z1/2/3	
30s	Z4/5/6
20s	Z1
Repeat x 6	
2 Minutes Recovery	Z1
30s	Z4/5/6
20s	Z1
Repeat x 6	
2 Minutes Recovery	Z1
30s	Z4/5/6
20s	Z1
Repeat x 6	

5 Minute Cool Down - Z1

No. 35

Duration: 26:45 Minutes.

Improves: Medium length sprints.

Good for: Continued development of Zone 6 ability.

Tip: Remember to have a drink close by as session durations get longer.

3 Minute Warm-up - Z1/2/3	
1 Minute	Z6
30s	Z1
Repeat x 4	
3 Minutes Recovery	Z1
2 Minutes	Z6
1 Minute	Z1
Repeat x 2	
3 Minutes Recovery	Z1
1 Minute	Z6
15s	Z1
Repeat x 3	

2 Minute Cool Down - Z1

<u>No. 36</u>

Duration: 27 minutes.

Improves: Standing sprints.

Good for: Combination of seated and standing Zone 6 efforts.

Tip: Aim to work the recovery period in Zone 3 rather than slipping into Zones 1 and 2.

5 Minute Warm-up - Z1/2/3	
30s Max effort, standing	Z6
30s Rest	Z1
30s Max effort, seated	Z6
30s Rest	Z1
30s Max effort, standing	Z6
30s Rest	Z1
8 Minutes Recovery	Z3
30s Max effort, standing	Z6
30s Rest	Z1
30s Max effort, seated	Z6
30s Rest	Z1
30s Max effort, standing	Z6
30s Rest	Z1

5 Minute Cool Down - Z1

No. 37

Duration: 28 minutes.

Improves: Short length climbing ability.

Good for: Longer duration standing intervals.

Tip: When standing pedal at a cadence, you find most comfortable due to the increased effort required when standing.

10 Minute Warm-up - Z1/2/3	
2 Minute Standing	Z5
1 Minute Seated	Z3/4
Repeat x 3	
20s Seated	Z5
10s Recovery	Z1
Repeat x 6	
30s Sprint	Z6
30s Recovery	Z1
Repeat x 6	
20s Seated	Z5
10s Recovery	Z1
Repeat x 6	

5 Minute Cool Down - Z1

No. 38

Duration: 29 minutes.

Improves: Sprinting.

Good for: Repeated Zone 6 short efforts.

Tip: Ensure you are firmly in Zone 1 during recovery due to high volume of Zone 6 work.

2 Minute Warm-up - Z1/2/3	
30s	Z6
30s	Z1
Repeat x 5	
3 Minute Recovery	Z1
30s	Z6
30s	Z1
Repeat 30s Intervals x 5	
2 Minute Recovery	Z1
30s	Z6
30s	Z1
Repeat 30s Intervals x 5	
1 Minute Recovery	
30s	Z6
30s	Z1
Repeat 30s Intervals x 5	

2 Minute Cool Down - Z1

No. 39

Duration: 29 minutes.

Improves: Sprinting and time trailing.

Good for: Work through training zones in one single effort with no recovery.

Tip: In the first two effort zones, the aim is to progress through the training zones finishing in the most difficult zone (i.e. in a 3-minute interval: 1 minute Z3, 1 minute Z4, 1 minute Z5).

5 Minute Warm-up - Z1/2/3	
3 Minutes	Z3/4/5
1 Minute Recovery	Z2
6 Minutes	Z3/4/5
2 Minutes Recovery	Z2
20s	Z6
10s	Z1
Repeat 20 + 10s Intervals x 8	
2 Minutes Recovery	Z2
20s	Z6
10s	Z1
Repeat 20 + 10s Intervals x 8	

5 Minute Cool Down - Z1

No. 40

Duration: 29:30 minutes.

Improves: Long duration sprints.

Good for: Long duration Zone 6 work.

Tip: Enjoy your time in the recovery zone.

5 Minute Warm-up - Z1/2/3	
90s	Max effort as close to Z6 as possible
90s Recovery	Z1
Repeat x 3	
2 minute recovery	Z1

Repeat 90s efforts with 2 Minute recovery x 3

5 Minute Cool Down - Z1

No. 41

Duration: 30 minutes.

Improves: Repetitive short climbs.

Good for: Maintaining effort while working near maximal intensity. This is the same programme as No. 2, but effort zones are in reverse so Zone 6 efforts are required under fatigue.

Tip: You will need to avoid straying early into the next zone during efforts, otherwise Zone 6 efforts will not be completed at full potential power.

5 Minute Warm-up - Z1/2/3	
30s	Z4
20s	Z5
10s	Z6
30s	Z1
Repeat x 15	

5 Minute Cool Down - Z1

No. 42

Duration: 30 minutes.

Improves: Time trailing.

Good for: A combination of short and long intervals.

Tip: Gradually progress through Zone 3/5 in the first interval, ideally around equal time in each zone.

5 Minute Warm-up - Z1/2/3	
5 Minute progression	Z3 to Z5
30s	Z5/6
30s	Z1
Repeat 30s intervals x 6	
20s	Z5/6
20s	Z1
Repeat x 6	
15s	Z6
15s	Z1
Repeat x 6	
10s Max Sprint	Z6

5 Minute Cool Down - Z1

No. 43

Duration: 30 minutes.

Improves: Short climbs.

Good for: Combining sprint and standing efforts into one programme.

Tip: Work to the last Zone 6 effort, and after a 24 sprint, you will find it hard to fully commit at the end.

6 Minute Warm-up - Z1/2/3	
30s Standing Climb	Z5
30s	Z3
Repeat x 6	
15s	Z6
15s	Z1
Repeat x 12	
6 Minute	Z3
10s	Z6
20s	Z1
Repeat 10s + 20s Intervals x 12	

6 Minute Cool Down - Z1

<u>*No. 44*</u>

Duration: 30 minutes.

Improves: Sprinting.

Good for: Zone 6 short durations.

Tip: A simple but effective session, look to full rest during the recovery.

5 Minute Warm-up - Z1/2/3	
30s	Z6
1:30 Minute	Z1
Repeat x10	

5 Minute Cool Down - Z1

No. 45

Duration: 30 minutes.

Improves: Medium length climbing.

Good for: Longer high intensity efforts.

Tip: Remember to get gearings correct when moving from seated to standing positions.

5 Minute Warm-up - Z1/2/3	
1 Minute Standing	Z5
1 Minute Seated	Z3
Repeat x 5	
30s Standing	Z4
30s Seated	Z4
Repeat x 5	
1 Minute Standing	Z5
30s Sprint	Z6
30s Recovery	Z1
Repeat x 5	

5 Minute Cool Down - Z1

No. 46

Duration: 30 minutes.

Improves: Short length time trailing.

Good for: Long interval Zone 4 efforts, Zone 5 immediately after.

Tip: No repetition on the longer Zone 4 efforts.

5 Minute Warm-up - Z1/2/3	
30s	Z5
30s	Z1
Repeat x 5	
4 Minutes	Z4
30s	Z5
30s	Z1
Repeat 30s Intervals x 4	
3 minutes	Z4
30s	Z5
30s	Z1
Repeat 30s Intervals x 3	
2 minutes	Z4
30s	Z5
30s	Z1
Repeat 30s Intervals x 2	
1 minute	Z4
30s	Z5
30s	Z1
Repeat 30s Intervals x 1	

5 Minute Cool Down - Z1

No. 47

Duration: 30 minutes.

Improves: Short length time trailing.

Good for: Increasing duration Zone 6 efforts with reducing Zone 1.

Tip: Ensure early efforts are not moving into Zone 6.

5 Minute Warm-up - Z1/2/3	
Z5	Z1
15s	75s
20s	70s
25s	65s
30s	60s
35s	55s
40s	50s
45s	45s
50s	40s
55s	35s
60s	30s
65s	25s
70s	20s
75s	15s

5 Minute Cool Down - Z1

No. 48

Duration: 30 minutes.

Improves: Ability to perform short repeated attacks.

Good for: Repeated Zone 5 intervals with only Zone 2 rest in between.

Tip: The relatively long work-to-rest ratios mean working in Zone 2 following the work efforts is achievable.

5 Minute Warm-up - Z1/2/3	
30s	Z5
30s	Z2
Repeat x 2	
20s	Z5
40s	Z2
Repeat x 2	
10s	Z6
50s	Z2
Repeat x 2	
20s	Z5
40s	Z2
Repeat x 2	
30s	Z5
30s	Z2
Repeat x 2	
5 Minute Rest	Z1
Repeat Whole Above x 2	

5 Minute Cool Down - Z1

No. 49

Duration: 30 minutes.

Improves: Short length time trailing.

Good for: Sustained duration workout with no rest between training zones.

Tip: Prepare yourself for a very difficult session.

3 Minute Warm-up - Z1/2/3	
1 Minute	Z6
2 Minute	Z5
3 Minute	Z4+
4 Minute	Z4-
5 Minute	Z3
4 Minute	Z4-
3 Minute	Z4+
2 Minute	Z5
1 Minute	Z6

2 Minute Cool Down - Z1

No. 50

Duration: 30 minutes.

Improves: Short length time trailing.

Good for: Medium length session working from Zone 3 to 6.

Tip: The pyramid structure aims to fatigue you early, so bear this in mind and don't go too hard early on, as you have to repeat the high intensity zones right at the end of the session.

4 Minute Warm-up - Z1/2/3	
1 Minute	Z6
2 Minutes	Z5
4 Minutes	Z4
8 Minutes	Z3
4 Minutes	Z4
2 Minutes	Z5
1 Minute	Z6

4 Minute Cool Down - Z1

8

Programmes - 31-1 Hour

Introduction of longer sustained efforts, with more time spent in Zones 4 and 5

No. 51

Duration: 34 minutes.

Improves: Short length time trailing or breakaway riding.

Good for: Working Z5/4 endurance.

Tip: This session is best completed following a period of rest due to the high intensity of the session.

5 Minute warm-up - Z1/2/3	
5 Minutes	Z5
15s Standing End of each Minute	Z5
1 minute Recovery	Z1
Repeat x 4	

5 Minute Cool Down - Z2/1

No. 52

Duration: 35 minutes.

Improves: Sprinting.

Good for: Medium length Zone 6 with minimal work to rest ratio.

Tip: After the first set of 45s, you may struggle to maintain Zone 6, so if you are struggling, drop to Zone 5.

5 Minutes Warm-up - Z1/2/3	
45s	Z6
15s	Z1
Repeat x 10	
5 Minutes Recovery	Z1
45s	Z5/6
15s	Z1
Repeat x 10	

5 Minute Cool Down - Z1

<u>*No. 53*</u>

Duration: 35 minutes.

Improves: Sprinting.

Good for: Improving Zone 6 sprint power.

Tip: Add into the middle of a steady Z2/3 ride, as long recovery periods allow for full maximal sprint power.

10 Minute warm-up - Z1/2/3	
15s Sprint	Z6
2:45 Minute	Z2
Repeat x 10	

10 Minute Cool Down - Z2/1

No. 54

Duration: 35:40 minutes.

Improves: Body ability to transition into different training zones.

Good for: Training in multiple zones.

Tip: In the 8-minute interval gradually move up from Zone 3 to Zone 5 over 4 minutes and then gradually drop down back to Zone 3. Also for the 6-minute interval gradually move up from Zone 4 to Zone 6.

5 Minute Warm-up - Z1/2/3	
8 Minutes	Z3/4/5/4/3
1 Minute Recovery	Z2
6 Minutes	Z4/5/6
1 Minute Recovery	Z2
30s	Z5 - Vo2 Max
10s	Z1
Repeat 30s + 10s Intervals x 10	
1 Minute Recovery	Z2
1 Minute	Z6
30s	Z1
Repeat 1 minute + 30s Interval x 2	

5 Minute Cool Down - Z1

No. 55

Duration: 39 minutes.

Improves: Medium length time trailing.

Good for: Pyramid ride moving through each training zone.

Tip: Long efforts with no rest progressing up and down through each training zone.

5 Minute Warm-up - Z1/2	
5 Minutes	Z3-
4 Minutes	Z3+
3 Minutes	Z4
2 Minutes	Z5
1 Minute	Z6
2 Minutes	Z5
3 Minutes	Z4
4 Minutes	Z3+
5 Minutes	Z3-

5 Minute Cool Down - Z1

No. 56

Duration: 40 minutes.

Improves: Repeated short climb ability.

Good for: Repeated Zone 5 efforts.

Tip: Ensure early 1-minute efforts are not in Zone 6 and each on remains in Zone 5.

5 Minute Warm-up - Z1/2/3	
1 Minute	Z5
30s	Z1
Repeat x 20	

5 Minute Cool Down - Z1

<u>*No. 57*</u>

Duration: 40 minutes.

Improves: Sprinting ability under low cadences.

Good for: Improving your ability to ride at low RPM, and apply sudden power bursts.

Tip: Avoid if you have troublesome knees.

5 Minute Warm-up - Z1/2 - RPM 100, Dropping by 10 Each Minute	
30 Minutes - RPM 70-80	Z3
15s Sprint every 5 Minutes	Z6

5 Minute Cool Down - Z1

No. 58

Duration: 40 minutes.

Improves: Tempo riding, Vo2 max riding, and sprinting.

Good for: Time working in Zones 3 up to 6.

Tip: On each of the 5 repetitions, gradually increase your training intensity through the zones (i.e. your first repetition will begin on Zone 3 + 4, and your 5th repetition should be Zone 5 + 6).

5 Minute Warm-up Z1/2/3	
1 Minute	Z3
1 Minute	Z4
1 Minute	Z3
1 Minute	Z4
1 minute	Z3
2 Minute Recovery	Z1

Repeat 5 times - Progressing through zones finishing in Z6

5 Minute Cool Down - Z1

No. 59

Duration: 40 minutes.

Improves: Aerobic and anaerobic training.

Good for: Exposure to both energy systems mentioned in the book and an ability to work through training zones in a short period of time.

Tip: Try to stick to the time periods stated rather than moving too early through the stated zones. Not doing this will reduce the time spent in one of the energy systems.

5 Minute warm-up - Z1/2	
1 Minute	Z2
1 Minute	Z3
1 Minute	Z4
1 Minute	Z5
1 Minute	Z6
5 Minute Recovery	Z1
Repeat x 3	

5 Minute Cool Down - Z2/1

No. 60

Duration: 41 minutes.

Improves: Short speed bursts.

Good for: Longer repeated intervals through Zone 4/5/6.

Tip: Move through the effort zones on each individual effort, (i.e. on the first two repetitions in Zone 4, next two repetitions in Zone 5, and next two repetitions in Zone 6).

5 Minute Warm-up - Z1/2/3	
60s	Z4/5/6
30s	Z1
Repeat x 6	
2 Minutes Recovery	Z1
60s	Z4/5/6
30s	Z1
Repeat x 6	
2 Minutes Recovery	Z1
60s	Z4/5/6
30s	Z1
Repeat x 6	

5 Minute Cool Down - Z1

No. 61

Duration: 43 minutes.

Improves: Medium length time trailing.

Good for: Progressions through Zone 3/4/5.

Tip: Each 2-minute block should be more difficult until on the last two minutes it is difficult to keep working at that speed.

5 Minute Warm-up - Z1/2/3	
2 Minutes	Z3+
2 Minutes	Z4
2 Minutes	Z5
3 Minute Recovery	Z1
Repeat x 2	

5 Minutes Cool Down - Z2/1

No. 62

Duration: 45 minutes.

Improves: Tempo riding and time trailing.

Good for: Great for simply improving muscular endurance and ability to repeat with small rest periods.

Tip: Ensure you are in Zone 1, not verging on Zone 2, during the rest periods due to the shortness of this session.

5 Minute Warm-up - Z1/2/3	
10 Minutes	Z4
2:30 Minutes Recovery	Z1
10 Minutes	Z4
2:30 Minutes Recovery	Z1
10 Minutes	Z4

5 Minute Cool Down - Z1

No. 63

Duration: 45 minutes.

Improves: Endurance riding, tempo riding, & fatigued sprints.

Good for: Accumulation of repeated attacks.

Tip: Stay in the suggested zones during the early 30s efforts.

5 Minute Warm-up - Z1/2/3	
30s	Z4
30s	Z1
Repeat x 6	
5 Minutes	Z3
30s	Z4+
30s	Z1
Repeat 30s intervals x 5	
4 minutes	Z3
30s	Z5
30s	Z1
Repeat 30s intervals x 4	
3 Minutes	Z3
30s	Z5+
30s	Z1
Repeat 30s intervals x 3	
2 minutes	Z3
30s	Z6
30s	Z1
Repeat 30s intervals x 2	
1 Minute	Z6

5 Minute Cool Down - Z2/1

No. 64

Duration: 45 minutes.

Improves: Short sprints.

Good for: Zone 5 efforts followed immediately by Zone 6.

Tip: Don't look to move into Zone 6 during the Zone 5 efforts when you're feeling fresh, otherwise your intensity will drop off during the later Zone 6 efforts.

5 Minute Warm-up - Z1/2/3	
1 Minute	Z5
1:30 Minute Recovery	Z1
Repeat x 4	
20s	Z6
10s	Z1
Repeat x 10	
5 Minute Recovery	Z1
Complete Whole Above Intervals x 2	
5 Minute Cool Down - Z1	

<u>No. 65</u>

Duration: 46 minutes.

Improves: Long sprinting ability.

Good for: Long duration efforts in Zone 5 + 6.

Tip: Dig deep as this session will work you hard thanks to the top end durations for these two zones.

5 Minute Warm-up - Z1/2/3	
2 Minutes	Z6
1 Minute Recovery	Z1
4 Minutes	Z5
2 Minutes Recovery	Z1
Repeat x 4	

5 Minute Cool Down - Z1

No. 66

Duration: 40 to 50 minutes.

Improves: Maximum duration sprinting ability.

Good for: Working without rest until exhaustion.

Advice: This session works on a progressive increase in difficulty, which is hard to describe in a table. After a 10 minute warm-up, keep cadence at 90 RPM and at every 30s, increase your perceived difficulty. Keep doing this progression until you are no longer able to maintain 90 RPM.

10 Minute warm-up - Z1/2/3	
5 to 10 Minutes - 90+ RPM Increase difficulty every 30s	Z4/5/6
5 minutes recovery after no longer able to maintain 90 RPM	Z1
Repeat x 2	

10 Minute Cool Down - Z2/1

No. 67

Duration: 52 minutes.

Improves: Cadence ability.

Good for: Cadence training at a tempo pace.

Tip: If the changes in cadence affect your knees, stick within your normal comfortable cadence.

10 Minute Warm-up - Z1/2	
1 Minute - 90 RPM	Z4
1 Minute - 110 RPM	Z4
Repeat x 6	
8 Minute Steady Riding	Z3
1 Minute - 120 RPM	Z4
1 Minute - 100 RPM	Z4
Repeat x 6	

10 Minute Cool Down - Z2/1

No. 68

Duration: 52 minutes.

Improves: Medium maximum effort hill climbs.

Good for: Working on maximum duration Z5 efforts.

Tip: Gradually progress through lower Zone 5 to upper Zone 5 in each effort.

10 Minute warm-up - Z1/2/3	
8 Minutes	Z5
4 Minutes Recovery	Z2
8 Minutes	Z5
4 Minutes Recovery	Z2
8 Minutes	Z5

10 Minute Cool Down - Z2/1

No. 69

Duration: 55 minutes.

Improves: Repeated sprinting over varying durations.

Good for: Improving Zone 6 power and ability to sustain this effort with little recovery.

Tip: For the first few repetitions, work within the lower classification of zone 6 and aim to maintain that level of effort.

10 Minute warm-up - Z1/2/3	
1 Minute	Z6
1 Recovery	Z1
30s	Z6
30s Recovery	Z1
15s	Z6
15s Recovery	Z1
X 10	

10 Minute Cool Down - Z2/1

No. 70

Duration: 55 minutes.

Improves: Medium length time trailing.

Good for: Zone 4 training.

Tip: Due to the simplicity of this ride, indoor riders may find this uninteresting, so I recommend completing this ride outdoors.

10 Minute Warm-up - Z1/2/3	
15 Minutes	Z4
5 Minutes	Z2
15 Minutes	Z4

15 Minute Cool Down - Z2/1

No. 71

Duration: 55 minutes.

Improves: Medium length time trials.

Good for: Working Zone 6 efforts when fatigued.

Tip: Aim to keep in mid-range Zone 4 so you're not fatigued in Zone 6 efforts.

10 Minute Warm-up Z1/2/3	
1:50 Minute	Z4
10s	Z6 - Sprint
Repeat x 10	
5 Minute Recovery	Z1
1:50 Minute	Z4
10s	Z6 - Sprint
Repeat x 10	

10 Minute Cool Down - Z1

No. 72

Duration: 55 *minutes.*

Improves: Medium length time trials.

Good for: Regular movements through tempo training zones.

Tip: If outdoors, it's easiest to do one straight road with little undulation.

15 Minute Warm-up Z1/2/3	
1 Minute	Z4
1 Minute	Z3+
Repeat x 15	

10 Minute Cool Down - Z1

No. 73

Duration: 56 minutes.

Improves: Ability to work at an anaerobic level.

Good for: Zone 6 efforts followed immediately by tempo Zone 4 work.

Tip: Although this session looks difficult, the high recovery periods make this session possible.

10 Minute Warm-up Z1/2/3	
30s	Z6
3:15 Minutes	Z4
15s	Z6
5 Minute Recovery	Z1
Repeat x 4	

10 Minute Cool Down - Z1

No. 74

Duration: 60 minutes.

Improves: Medium length time trials.

Good for: Improving the Zone 5 ability through working within your sweet spot.

Tip: Remember that the 'sweet spot' is 90% of your FTP.

10 Minute Warm-up - Z1/2/3	
5 Minute	Z5 - Sweet spot
10s Sprint 2:30 into interval	Z6
5 Minutes Recovery	Z2
Repeat x 4	

10 Minute Cool Down - Z1

No. 75

Duration: 60 minutes.

Improves: Medium length time trials.

Good for: Improving VO2 max.

Tip: Ensure you don't drop below Zone 4 in the 40s intervals, as this is high to allow minimal recovery for each VO2 effort and simulate multiple attacks if riding on the road.

10 Minute Warm-up - Z1/2/3	
40s	Z4
20s	Z5 - VO2
Repeat x 10	
5 Minutes Recovery	Z1
40s	Z4
20s	Z5 - VO2
Repeat x 10	
5 Minutes Recovery	Z1
40s	Z4
20s	Z5 - VO2
Repeat x 10	

10 Minute Cool Down - Z1/2

No. 76

Duration: 60 minutes.

Improves: Anaerobic tolerance.

Good for: Progressive training through maximum time possible in Zone 5.

Tip: Aim to hit threshold heart rate or power after five mins and finish right at limit of zone hour in the final minute of each effort.

10 Minute Warm-up - Z1/2/3	
10 Minute Progressive Effort	Lower Z4 to Upper Z5
10 Minutes Recovery	Z2
Repeat x 2	

10 Minute Cool Down - Z1

No. 77

Duration: 60 minutes.

Improves: Short sprints.

Good for: Maximal Zone 6 efforts with high rest-to-work ratio.

Tip: As you progress, increase work time to 20-30s.

15 Minute Warm-up Z1/2/3	
15s	Z6
45s	Z2
Repeat x 5	
5 Minute Recovery	Z2
Repeat x 5	

15 Minute Cool Down - Z2

No. 78

Duration: 60 minutes.

Improves: Medium length hill climbing.

Good for: Outdoor climbing ability.

Tip: Where possible, this is best completed outdoors on a steep climb.

10 Minute Warm-up Z1/2/3/4	
1 Minute	Z5/6
2 Minutes	Z1
Repeat x 5	
5 Minute Recovery	Z1
1 Minute	Z5/6
2 Minutes	Z1
Repeat x 5	

5 Minute Cool Down - Z1

No. 79

Duration: 60 minutes.

Improves: Time trials and sprint while fatigued.

Good for: Threshold efforts.

Tip: Early recovery periods in Zone 2 to later high zone work is completed in a pre-fatigued state.

4 Minute Warm-up Z1/2	
10 Minutes	Z4
5 Minutes Recovery	Z2
5 Minutes	Z5
1 Minute Recovery	Z2
5 Minutes	Z5
5 Minute Recovery	Z2
2 Minutes	Z5+
30s Recovery	Z1
2 Minutes	Z5+
30s Recovery	Z1
2 Minutes	Z5+
5 Minute Recovery	Z1
1 Minute	Z6
30s Recovery	Z1
Repeat 1 Minute and 30s Intervals x 6	

4 Minute Cool Down - Z1

No. 80

Duration: 60 minutes.

Improves: Short time trials.

Good for: Vo2 max training session.

Tip: This will improve your ability to go harder and faster in short bursts close to maximum effort.

10 Minute Warm-up - Z1/2	
3 Minutes	Z5 - Vo2
6 Minutes Recovery	Z2
Repeat x 5	

5 Minute Cool Down - Z2/1

9
Programmes - 1:01 Hour+

Longest sessions found in this book which draw on all training zones

No. 81

Duration: 64 minutes.

Improves: Cadence efficiency.

Good for: High intensity training at lower cadences.

Tip: Increase the cadence speed if you have painful knees.

10 Minute Warm-up - Z1/2/3	
1 Minute - 70 RPM	Z6
2 Minute Recovery	Z1
2 Minute - 70 RPM	Z5
2 Minutes Recovery	Z1
3 Minutes - 70 RPM	Z5
2 Minutes Recovery	Z1
4 Minutes - 70 RPM	Z5
2 Minutes Recovery	Z1
5 Minutes - 70 RPM	Z4
2 Minutes Recovery	Z1
4 Minutes - 70 RPM	Z5
2 Minutes Recovery	Z1
3 Minutes - 70 RPM	Z5
2 Minutes Recovery	Z1
2 Minute - 70 RPM	Z5
2 Minutes Recovery	Z1
1 Minute - 70 RPM	Z6

10 Minute Cool Down - Z1

No. 82

Duration: 70 minutes.

Improves: Long hill climbing.

Good for: Increasing functional threshold power.

Tip: If you are completing this programme outdoors, try to find a relatively flat route.

10 Minute Warm-up - Z1/2/3	
20 Minutes	FTP
10 Minutes Recovery	Z2
Repeat x 2	

10 Minute Cool Down - Z2/1

No. 83

Duration: 70 minutes.

Improves: Repeated short efforts.

Good for: Threshold training for improving your ability to work slightly above and below threshold effort for medium length intervals.

Tip: Recovery is in Z2 to maintain slight effort instead of near complete rest.

20 Minute Warm-up - Z1/2/3	
1 Minute	Z5 - Vo2
1 Minute	Z4 - Threshold
1 Minute	Z3 - Tempo
1 Minute	Z4 - Threshold
1 Minute	Z5 - Vo2
5 Minute Recovery	Z2
Repeat x 4	

10 Minute Cool Down - Z2/1

No. 84

Duration: 70 minutes.

Improves: Cadence efficiency.

Good for: Cadence work with training at tempo speed.

Tip: 2 x 20 minute blocks of cadence drills, after completing the 60-70 RPM 2 minutes return to 2 minutes 100-110 RPM.

5 Minute Warm-up Z1/2/3	
2 Minutes - 100-110	Z4
2 Minutes - 90-100 RPM	Z4
2 Minutes - 80-90 RPM	Z4
2 Minutes - 70-80 RPM	Z4
2 Minutes - 60-70 RPM	Z4
Repeat until 20 minute Block Complete	
10 Minutes Recovery	Z1
Repeat Above x 2	

5 Minute Cool Down - Z2/1

No. 85

Duration: 70 minutes.

Improves: Short hill climbing.

Good for: Being able to complete repeat short climbs in quick succession without seeing performance drop off.

Tip: Best completed on a hill that lasts longer than 5 minutes. After each interval, you can roll down the hill and repeat, aiming on each interval to finish the 5 minutes at the same point on the hill and not drop off.

10 Minute Warm-up - Z1/2/3/4	
5 Minutes	Z5
5 Minutes	Z1
Repeat x 5	

10 Minute Cool Down - Z1

<u>*No. 86*</u>

Duration: 75 minutes.

Improves: Endurance riding.

Good for: Endurance riding with small high intensity efforts.

Tip: Remember to bring adequate fluid and food due to the length of the programme.

10 Minute Warm-up - Z2	
5 Minutes	Z3
1 Minute	Z5
4 Minutes	Z4
5 Minutes Recovery	Z1
Repeat x 5	

10 Minute Cool Down - Z2/1

No. 87

Duration: 75:45 minutes.

Improves: Long duration sprints.

Good for: Increasing duration Zone 6 efforts.

Tip: Where possible, best completed outdoors on a steep climb.

10 Minute Warm-up Z1/2	
1 Minute	Z6
2 minute Recovery	Z1
Repeat x 5	
5 Minute Recovery	Z1
1:15 Minute	Z6
2 Minute Recovery	Z1
Repeat x 5	
5 Minute Recovery	Z1
1:30 Minute	Z6
2 Minute Recovery	Z1
Repeat x 5	

5 Minute Cool Down - Z2/1

No. 88

Duration: 77 minutes.

Improves: Seated and standing sprints.

Good for: Standing start sprints and sprints while moving.

Tip: In the 3rd set of sprints, there are no parameters to stick to; they are simply all-out sprints to your preferred cadence.

20 Minutes Warm-up - Z1/2/3	
15s - Stationary Start Sprint - RPM Below 100	Z6
2 Minutes Recovery	Z1
Repeat x 4	
10 Minutes Recovery	Z2
15s - Rolling Start Sprint - RPM Below 120+	Z6
2 Minutes Recovery	Z1
Repeat x 4	
10 Minutes Recovery	Z1
15s - Any RPM	Z6
2 Minutes Recovery	Z1
Repeat x 4	

10 Minutes Cool Down - Z2/1

No. 89

Duration: 80 minutes.

Improves: Long hill climbing ability.

Good for: Long climbs and working within your lactate tolerance. The bursts are useful for when you meet an increase in gradient.

Tip: Bursts should be around 120-150% FTP.

20 Minute Warm-up - Z1/2/3	
5 Minutes	Z1/2
20 Minutes	Z4 - Sweet spot
Every 2 Minutes 10s Saddle Burst	Z5
15 Minutes recovery	Z2
5 Minutes	Z1/2
20 Minutes	Z4 - Sweet spot
Every 2 Minutes 10s Saddle Burst	Z5

10 Minute Cool Down - Z2/1

No. 90

Duration: 80 minutes.

Improves: Time trials with short sprints.

Good for: Zone 4 training with Zone 6 sprints.

Tip: Following the sprints within Zone 4's 20 minutes, aim to return straight to this speed rather than momentarily dropping to Zone 3/2.

20 Minute Warm-up - Z2/3	
20 Minutes	Z4
15s Every 5 Minutes in 20 Minute Interval	Z6
10 Minutes Recovery	Z2
20 Minutes	Z4
15s Every 5 Minutes in 20 Minute Interval	Z6

10 Minute Cool Down - Z2/1

No. 91

Duration: 80 minutes.

Improves: Cadence efficiency.

Good for: Leg strength by dropping your cadence, forcing you to push harder on the pedals to hit the required power or heart rate. This will encourage your leg muscles to adapt and grow stronger.

Tip: Avoid if you have knee issues.

10 Minute Warm-up Z1/2	
10 Minutes - 60 RPM	Z3
5 Minutes - 90-100 RPM	Z2
10 Minutes - 55 RPM	Z3
5 Minutes - 90-100 RPM	Z2
10 Minutes - 50 RPM	Z3

10-15 Minute Cool Down - Z2/1

<u>*No. 92*</u>

Duration: 80 minutes.

Improves: Tempo riding following short sprints.

Good for: Zone 4, 5, and 6 work with minimal recovery periods.

Tip: Trying to complete 3-minute efforts in Zone 5 will not be possible, so ensure these are done within Zone 4.

5 Minute Warm-up - Z1/2	
2 Minute	Z5
3 Minutes	Z4
15s	Z6
3 Minutes	Z4
15s	Z6
3 Minutes	Z4
15s	Z6
3 Minutes	Z4
15s	Z6
10 Minutes Recovery	Z1
Repeat Another x 2	

10 Minute Cool Down - Z2/1

No. 93

Duration: 80:30 minutes.

Improves: Time trials at a variety of cadence speeds.

Good for: Medium length Zone 5 work.

Tip: Ensure you gradually move through your cadence speeds during 3-minute intervals.

10 Minute Warm-up - Z1/2/3	
3 Minutes	Z5
30s Rest	Z1
Move between 80/90/100/110 RPM each 3 Minute Block	
Repeat x 7	
4 Minute Recovery	Z1
4 Minutes	Z5
30s Rest	Z1
Move between 80/90/100 RPM each 3 Minute Block	
Repeat 4 Minute and 30s rest x 5	
3 Minute Recovery	Z1
5 Minute	Z4/5
30s Recovery	Z1
Self-Selected RPM	
Repeat 5 Minute and 30s rest x 3	

10 Minute Cool Down - Z1

<u>*No. 94*</u>

Duration: 88 minutes.

Improves: Short hill climb efforts.

Good for: Improving Zone 5 ability.

Tip: Your heart rate when moving from Zone 5 to 3 won't adapt quickly enough for you to know if you're in Zone 3, so you will have to either use power or RPE.

20 Minutes Warm-up - Z1/2/3	
50s	Z5 - Sweet spot
10s	Z3
Repeat x 8	
6 Minute Recovery	Z1
Repeat Whole Programme x 5	

10 Minute Cool Down - Z1

No. 95

Duration: 94 minutes.

Improves: Cadence efficiency.

Good for: Low and high cadence work within Zones 4 & 5.

Tip: Equal work-to-rest ratios means you should be able to complete this within the correct zones.

20 Minute Warm-up Z1/2/3	
6 Minutes - 60-70 RPM	Z4
2 Minutes - 110-120 RPM	Z5
8 Minutes Recovery	Z2
Repeat x 4	

10 Minute Cool Down - Z1

No. 96

Duration: 105 minutes.

Improves: Endurance riding.

Good for: Endurance with end progressions to higher zones.

Tip: Easiest to pace using HR.

1 Hour	Z2
15 Minutes	Z3
15 Minutes	Z4
10 Minutes	Z5

5 Minutes Cool Down - Z1

No. 97

Duration: 110 minutes.

Improves: Long time trials.

Good for: Training within your sweet spot zone for longer durations.

Tip: As you progress, you can increase the number of Zone 6 efforts during the 20 minute intervals.

20 Minute Warm-up - Z1/2	
20 Minute	Z4/5 - Sweet spot
10s Sprint Every 5 Minutes	Z6
10 Minute Recovery	Z2
Repeat x 3	

10 Minute Cool Down - Z1

No. 98

Duration: 120 minutes.

Improves: Endurance and time trial ability.

Good for: Basic endurance work with some Zone 5 effort.

Tip: Best completed outside due to the little variance in the programme.

30 Minute Warm-up - Z2	
5 Minutes	Z5
6 Minutes	Z3
Repeat x 5	

30 Minutes Cool Down - Z2

No. 99

Duration: 120 minutes.

Improves: Endurance and tempo riding.

Good for: Ability to switch repeatedly between low level training zones.

Tip: If training indoors or no climbs of this length are in your area, complete efforts at a higher gear than you would normally ride. If you complete this on the same road every time, you can see if you progress further down the road, or go further on your indoor trainer.

30 Minutes Warm-up - Z2	
10 Minutes	Z3/4
5 Minutes Recovery	Z1/2
Repeat x 4	

15 Minutes Cool Down - Z2/1

<u>*No. 100*</u>

Duration: 140 minutes.

Improves: Endurance and long duration climbing ability.

Good for: Tempo riding in Zone 4.

Tip: If outside, look for an easy route. As you progress, look to increase Z4 blocks to 45-60 min.

30 Minute Warm-up - Z1/2	
30 Minutes	Z4
1 Hour	Z2/3
30 Minutes	Z4

10 Minute Cool Down - Z1/2

No. 101

Duration: 150 minutes.

Improves: Endurance riding.

Good for: Endurance riding in Zone 2 and 3.

Tip: Although this is one of the boring programmes, this one is great for building long ride endurance and getting to see the countryside. Remember to have food and water available.

30 Minute Warm-up - Z1	
30 Minute	Z2
30 Minute	Z3
30 Minute	Z2

30 Minute Cool Down - Z1

10
Fitness Tests

In the section below, you will find a small selection of fitness tests that can be used to monitor your ongoing fitness progressions. Unfortunately, most tests below use power, simply due to the objective measure it is able to produce.

Max Power

This test's main aim is to find your maximal possible power.

Method: Unfortunately, this test needs to be completed on a power meter fitted bike, turbo trainer or stationary bike. You will complete one max 6-second sprint. From this, you must record your maximum power and average power for the 6 seconds.

5 Minute Warm-up - Z1/2/3/4 - Complete One 6s Surge Every Minute	
6s	Z6+

5 Minute Cool Down - Z2/1

Maximum Minute Power + HR Max

This test is ideal for finding the maximum amount of power you can sustain in one minute and also for finding a max heart rate.

Method: Put simply, this is one maximum effort over 3 minutes, so gauge your effort in the first period, as you will run out of power in the last minute.

You can then use a cycling computer to assess what the maximum average power you held for one minute was and what max heart rate you achieved was.

The best systems for this would be a new Garmin cycling computer or a watt bike.

5 Minute Warm-up Z1/2/3/4	
3 Minutes	Z6

5 Minute Cool Down - Z2/1

Functional Threshold Power and/or HR

This is one of the most recognised methods for testing FTP for power and HR.

Method: This test looks to find the maximum power you are able to sustain for 20 minutes. It is important to pace this session well again, or else you will see a big drop off for the later periods of the test. After completing the test, you simply get a 20 minute average power and multiply it by 0.95 to give you your FTP.

10 Minute Warm-up Z1/2/3/4	
20 Minutes	Z4+

5 Minute Cool Down - Z2/1

Simple Hill Climb

This test is great for those without power meters and HR belts. It can be modified to monitor short or long distance duration and all you need is a hill. It is also one of the least scientific methods of monitoring fitness due to the immeasurable effects of wind, rain, heat, etc.

Method: On your selected hill, you will choose a duration you wish to work toward. The length of your chosen duration will decide which zone you are working in.

Once your warm-up is complete, you simply ride up the hill for your chosen duration. When time is up, stop and note how far you have travelled. Next time you test your fitness, you can see if you have improved your distance or fallen short.

10 Minute Warm-up Z1/2/3/4	
3 - 20 Minutes	Z3 - 4 - 5 - 6

10 Minute Cool Down - Z2/1

Acknowledgments

I would like to thank all the people who have inspired and given their time to help me write this book, without them this would not have been possible. Thank you to Michelle for your patience with my many hours cycling which have inspired me to write this book and your help and advice proof reading.

I would like to thank Dean Barber and Max Duffield for their help and guidance reading through the many grammatical errors and suggesting areas to add within the book which has added greatly to the quality found in the book. Thanks to Jack Powley for being present during the lightbulb moment when the idea for this book appeared during one of our many sweaty watt bike training sessions, and of course his help and inspiration for some sessions found in the book.

Finally, to my wonderful parents, thank you for the support you have given to me throughout my life which has allowed me to be in the position to be able to write a book such as this.

Glossary

Road Bike - This type of bike is specifically designed for riding primarily on paved roads, with designed with emphasis on speed.

Mountain Bike - This type of bike is specifically designed for riding off-road on rocky, muddy, and slippery terrain. These bikes are often built with stronger and heavier frames than a road bike.

Cyclocross Bike - This bike is generally a combination of a road and mountain bike, with narrow wheels like a road bike and tread like a mountain bike. They are best suited to muddy and grassy terrain.

Static Bike - This form of bike has no capability to actually move and cannot be used for transportation. However, they work in exactly the same way as an outdoor bike and can be used in the same way as a normal bike.

Turbo Trainer - This is a static machine you attach to the rear wheel of a bike. The machine allows the user to pedal while not moving, essentially turning the bike into a static bike. A resistance can be applied to make riding harder if necessary.

Time Trials - These are events where cyclists aim to cover a set distance, on a set course, on their own within the fastest possible time. Cyclists ride individually and usually set off at one minute intervals.

Road Race - This is a competitive event which generally takes place on open roads or a track. Ranging from 20 to 100+ participants, riders will race over the set distance, laps, or time trying to cross the finish line first.

Hill Climb - Similar to a time trial, riders are riding for their best possible time, usually setting off in one-minute intervals. Hill climbs are all on uphill roads with steep or shallow gradients.

Heart Rate - This is the number of times your heart beats within one minute. This figure over one minute is normally described as beats per minute (BPM). It is often used as an indication of the level of exertion.

Power - This is the amount of force and velocity applied to the pedals during cycling and is expressed as a watt. It is used as a measure of intensity.

Watts - This is the name given to express the power provided from the cyclist to the pedals. It is an objective number and can be compared with professional cyclists as a direct contrast.

RPE - This stands for rated perceived exertion. It is a method of measuring the level of exertion. It is measured on a 10-point scale, with 0 being rest and 10 being a maximal effort.

Training Plans - This is an organised system that details a set of rides an individual will follow in order to achieve a goal in the future (e.g. riding race, hill climb, time trial).

Periodisation - This is a more precise form of a training plan that will target being at the peak of physical fitness for certain competitions throughout one or more years. It splits the athletes programme into specific training, competition and recovery periods.

Climbing - This is where a cyclist rides uphill, whether it's small hills or large mountains where riders can climb 3,000 ft. Short climbs are typically suited to stronger, more physical riders, whereas long climbs are best suited to lighter riders.

Sprinting - This is where a rider accelerates and travels at their maximum speed in a short period of time. It can be done uphill, downhill, and on flat terrain. It is most commonly seen at the end of road races when riders are moving to the line.

Functional Threshold - This is the best possible effort a rider is able to produce over a 40 minute to 1 hour ride. This type of effort is usually seen when cyclists are riding in time trials.

Sweet Spot - A specific training zone which is at 90% of functional threshold power/HR, it aims to produce the optimum training level without inducing long periods of fatigue through the following days.

VO2 Max - The maximum rate your body (heart, lungs and muscles) can use oxygen during intense exercise over one minute. It is commonly tested and then used as an indicator of fitness.

Aerobic System - This is one of the energy systems the human body utilises during exercise. As the name suggests, it utilises oxygen to help produce energy and is predominantly used in endurance-based activities.

Anaerobic System - This is another of the energy systems which the human body uses to produce energy but does not require oxygen during exercise. This energy system is used during short, intense bursts of activity.

High Intensity Interval Training - A form of training completed over a relatively short period of time. However, to get effective physiological changes, exercise is completed at a high intensity with relatively short rest periods.

Recovery - This is the act of rest following periods of training. Recovery allows the body to adapt to the physiological strain being placed upon it. Without recovery, big improvements in fitness will not occur.

Cadence - Also referred to as RPM, this is the speed in which pedals are turned when cycling. Cadence is often a self-selected speed, usually ranging from 70-100 RPM. Pedaling too slowly or too fast may cause knee, ankle or back pain.

Cycling Computers – These are devices usually placed upon bike handlebars that provide information related to your bike session (e.g. speed, cadence, time, etc.). They may be GPS-enabled, allowing tracking of distance, height gain, where you have travelled, etc.

Bib Shorts - These are specifically designed to allow for a more comfortable riding experience. They typically come with a padded area that sits above the saddle for comfort, and they can be designed for winter and summer to allow riding in all conditions.

Training Zones - These indicate the intensity of your training. Each zone is set to a specific intensity and allows a selective process to measure and control how hard to ride during a training session.

Printed in Great Britain
by Amazon